W9-AVI-716

TRAVEL THE WORLD TO HELP ANIMALS WITH ...

SCIENTISTS *in* ACTION!

Big-Animal Vets!

MC

SCIENTISTS in ACTION!

Archaeologists!

Astronauts!

Big-Animal Vets!

Biomedical Engineers!

Civil Engineers!

Climatologists!

Crime Scene Techs!

Cyber Spy Hunters!

Marine Biologists!

Robot Builders!

Big-Animal Vets!

By Mari Rich

Mason Crest
450 Parkway Drive, Suite D
Broomall, PA 19008
www.masoncrest.com

Printed and bound in the United States of America.

Series ISBN: 978-1-4222-3416-7
Hardback ISBN: 978-1-4222-3419-8
EBook ISBN: 978-1-4222-8480-3

First printing
1 3 5 7 9 8 6 4 2

Produced by Shoreline Publishing Group LLC
Santa Barbara, California
Editorial Director: James Buckley Jr.
Designer: Tom Carling, Carling Design Inc.
Production: Sandy Gordon
www.shorelinepublishing.com
Cover image: Jessie Cohen/Smithsonian National Zoo/Newscom

Library of Congress Cataloging-in-Publication Data
Rich, Mari, author.
      Big-animal vets / by Mari Rich.
      pages cm. -- (Scientists in action!)
      Includes bibliographical references and index.
ISBN 978-1-4222-3419-8 (hardback : alk. paper) -- ISBN 978-1-4222-3416-7 (series) -- ISBN 978-1-4222-8480-3 (ebook) 1. Veterinary medicine--Juvenile literature. 2. Veterinarians--Juvenile literature. 3. Exotic animals--Treatment--Juvenile literature. 4. Wildlife diseases--Juvenile literature. I. Title.
SF756.R525 2015
636.089--dc23
                                2015004674

Contents

Key Icons to Look For

Words to Understand: These words with their easy-to-understand definitions will increase the reader's understanding of the text, while building vocabulary skills.

Sidebars: This boxed material within the main text allows readers to build knowledge, gain insights, explore possibilities, and broaden their perspectives by weaving together additional information to provide realistic and holistic perspectives.

Research Projects: Readers are pointed toward areas of further inquiry connected to each chapter. Suggestions are provided for projects that encourage deeper research and analysis.

Text-Dependent Questions: These questions send the reader back to the text for more careful attention to the evidence presented here.

Series Glossary of Key Terms: This back-of-the-book glossary contains terminology used throughout this series. Words found here increase the reader's ability to read and comprehend higher-level books and articles in this field.

Action!

eep in the African jungle, Dr. Mike Cranfield was just trying to help—but the huge, angry silverback gorilla staring him down didn't know that. Cranfield was a big-animal veterinarian trying to care for a sick baby gorilla. The silverback thought the vet was a threat. The next minutes would determine whether Cranfield would become a patient himself. An angry silverback is one of the most dangerous animals around. When you devote your life to caring for animals in the wild, though, facing angry patients is part of the job.

Moments before the adult gorilla appeared, Cranfield cradled a sick three-week-old mountain gorilla gently in his arms. Its mother slept peacefully at

WORDS TO UNDERSTAND

anesthesia   medicine that puts a patient to sleep for an operation or other medical procedure

poachers   people who capture or kill wild animals illegally

primate   a type of four-limbed mammal with a developed brain; includes humans, apes, and monkeys

7

his feet. Cranfield had shot the mother with a dart carrying a safe tranquilizer that put her to sleep. That allowed Cranfield to approach the baby gorilla safely. They were on a misty hillside in Uganda's Bwindi Impenetrable National Park. The vet was there as part of a mission by the Gorilla Doctors.

The Gorilla Docs, as many people know them, take care of sick and injured gorillas that live in the national parks of Rwanda, Uganda, and the Democratic Republic of Congo (DRC), the only three countries where mountain gorillas live. The Gorilla Docs believe that the health and well-being of every single mountain gorilla is extremely important because there are only about 800 of them alive today in the entire world.

At least twice a week, the Gorilla Docs go out into the bush to see the gorillas and monitor their condition. Does everyone look healthy? Do any of them have visible skin problems or wounds? Sometimes the gorillas get caught in snares or traps set by **poachers**. When that happens, the vets and their helpers must release the trapped gorillas.

One gorilla living in Rwanda's Volcanoes National Park was even caught in a snare twice, once when he was four years old and once when he was seven. Zirikana, as he had been named, was fortunate to escape serious injury, but other gorillas have not been quite as lucky; the Gorilla Docs have been forced to amputate if an arm or leg is too badly mangled.

Doing complex surgery is always hard, but it's even harder out in the field. The veterinarians must carry all the equipment they might need, including an **anesthesia** machine and heavy monitors, up steep hillsides and over slippery terrain. Imagine setting up an entire operating room in a forest clearing!

It's a tough job, but Cranfield, who was born in Canada, can't imagine doing anything else. For almost as long as he can remember, he has wanted to work with wild animals. As a college student, he helped out at a small zoo in Ontario, and after he finished veterinary school,

After capturing the baby gorilla, Dr. Cranfield uses a portable anesthesia machine to make sure the animal is safely sleeping before doing any procedures.

Given the size and potential danger of gorillas, Dr. Cranfield (right) has a team of helpers with him to make sure that they and the animal are safe throughout the operation.

he traveled to Japan to help set up an animal park there. He became a Gorilla Doc in 1999, and his many years of experience taught him just what to do on that misty morning he found himself within inches of the angry silverback.

Named for the stripe of silvery-gray fur they develop across their backs when they reach maturity, male mountain gorillas can weigh almost 500 pounds and are said to have six times the strength of the average human. Gorillas live in troops, and each troop has a dominant silverback that serves as a leader and protector. Although mountain gorillas are usually gentle and calm, this massive silverback, now standing close enough so that Cranfield could feel its warm breath on his face, was visibly displeased to see that the doctor was holding a young gorilla. The silverback had no way of knowing that Cranfield was a doctor.

As the silverback advanced, Cranfield carefully placed the infant gorilla on the ground, and then backed away. His Ugandan helpers rushed in. Positioning themselves between the vet and the silverback, they thumped the ground with sticks, gently coaxing the male back into the forest. Cranfield would have to return the next day to examine the baby, a prospect that he didn't mind. When you're working among troops of mountain gorillas, which can have more than a dozen members, you're often outside of your comfort zone, he says. That can be exciting, and it also can be very satisfying.

When Cranfield saves a baby from a snare, treats a silverback's infection, or collects blood samples that help researchers discover more about **primate** health, he knows he has one of the best, most important jobs in the world.

The Scientists and Their Science

ny veterinarian will tell you that they love animals. If you want to be a wildlife vet, however, it's not enough simply to be an animal lover. You also have to be hard-working, quick-thinking, and, above all, adventurous. Chances are that no two days will be exactly alike. Whether they choose to protect wildlife in a foreign country such as Mike Cranfield does, look after the inhabitants of an animal sanctuary, work in a zoo, or ensure that performing animals are healthy and well cared for, wildlife vets never know what will await them when they get out of bed.

WORDS TO UNDERSTAND

anatomy   a branch of knowledge that deals with the structure of organisms

gore   to pierce or wound with something pointed

maul   to attack and injure someone in a way that cuts or tears skin

pharmacology   the study of drugs—their composition, effects, and use in medicine

specialize   to focus your efforts on one particular activity or field

13

Dr. Jeremiah Poghon heads a veterinary unit in the Tsavo region of Kenya for the David Sheldrick Wildlife Trust, a group dedicated to helping endangered African species. He has to be ready to swing into action at a moment's notice because if he delays, the injured animal might leave the area, making itself hard to find. If the injury is bad enough, the animal might die before the mobile unit arrives. Dr. Poghon might be called upon to aid a water buffalo that has fallen into a deep hole, attach a radio collar to a lioness so that researchers can study her, or treat a baby elephant that has been attacked by hyenas.

Some vets **specialize** in just one species of animal, but that doesn't mean their days are dull. Dr. Tang Chunxiang is the senior vet at the China Conservation and Research Center for the Giant Panda, and his tasks often include rushing out to the field to rescue an injured animal, checking on patients in the center's massive panda hospital, and overseeing health research in the lab. That's a lot of duties, but each one is aimed at protecting the endangered creatures. (There are only about 1,600 giant pandas left in the world!)

Is It Dangerous?

Most wildlife veterinarians go their entire careers without getting badly hurt, but that's because they're very careful. Elephants, rhinos, and other animals are many times larger than the humans taking care of them. Some vets are fond of the saying, "If it has a mouth, it can bite." You could add that if it has a horn or tusks it can **gore** you, if it has claws it can **maul** you, and if it has legs, it can chase you.

Wildlife vets spend years learning how to safely restrain or sedate their patients before examining them. In the wild, they use dart guns

Vets working in China with panda babies don't have to worry about their safety too much, but those working with adult pandas need to be on their guard.

or blowpipes to give sleep drugs to larger animals, such as elephants, lions, giraffes, and gorillas. Smaller animals can sometimes be caught using nets or ropes. Even after an animal seems under control, however, danger can still lurk. Dr. Angela Lassiter, who works at the Carolina Tiger Rescue sanctuary, says that big cats, particularly leopards and cougars, react unpredictably to anesthesia. They sometimes don't give any warning signs when they are about to wake up. That's why wildlife vets always have teams of helpers, ready to jump in if things go wrong.

This vet working with a tiger has to make sure the animal is safely sedated before entering the enclosure to check its skin for cuts, scrapes, or disease.

Having a big cat wake up in the middle of a medical procedure is not the scariest situation Dr. Lassiter has ever been in. The sanctuary sometimes takes in big cats that have been taken away from people who have purchased them illegally. So from time to time she has to deal with very hostile humans who ignored the fact that keeping wild animals as pets can be dangerous and is illegal.

Luckily, veterinarians have an even more important tool than anesthesia or rope restraints: common sense! They remain aware of the dangers at all times and use their knowledge of animal behavior to avoid trouble. For example, a smart wildlife vet will never make direct eye contact with a male gorilla—that might be considered a direct challenge. The vet will never get between a super-protective mother grizzly bear and her cubs. As long as you're careful, most will tell you, the rewards of working with such wonderful animals far outweigh the risks.

A Wild Education

Veterinarians complete several years of formal training before treating an animal. All vets first earn a four-year college degree. They take many science and math classes before going to veterinary school. Of course, all vets will also tell you they never stop learning more about the animals they treat.

There are only 28 veterinary schools in the United States. Schools get many more applicants than they have room for each year, so it isn't unusual for a future vet to be turned down at first. Once admitted to veterinary school, expect to work really hard. At first, you will spend most of your time in the classroom. You may feel disappointed that you're not working with animals right away, but you still have a lot to learn about subjects

History Lesson

As far back as 3000 BCE, people have been taking care of animals. Tablets from the ancient land of Mesopotamia mention a man named Urlugaledinna, who was "an expert in healing animals."

The world's first veterinary school was founded in 1761 in Lyon, France, by Claude Bourgelat. Bourgelat had been a lawyer but decided to become a veterinarian after he witnessed many cows in France getting sick and dying. Bourgelat was an expert horseman, so he was very familiar with animals.

The first veterinarians in the United States were trained at Cornell University beginning in 1876. Today, more than 105,000 people work as veterinarians in the United States and Canada.

such as **anatomy**, nutrition, and **pharmacology**. By the fourth year in veterinary school, students are working alongside teachers with real patients. Every veterinary student works with pets such as cats and dogs, larger domestic animals including horses and cows, and all kinds of wildlife. Only then do they pick an area in which to specialize.

If you pick wildlife, you may choose to study for up to three extra years in a program called a residency, which will give you the extra knowledge you need out in the field.

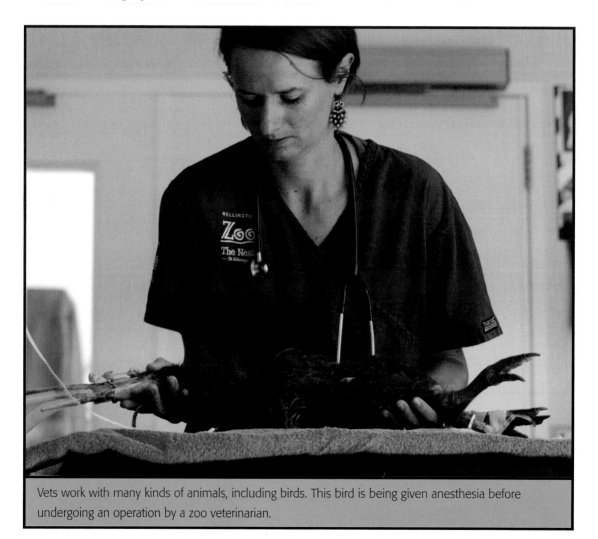

Vets work with many kinds of animals, including birds. This bird is being given anesthesia before undergoing an operation by a zoo veterinarian.

Visitors to a zoo might enjoy a tour given by a zoo volunteer who is studying to become a vet.

For students with an eye toward helping large wild animals, as opposed to cats and dogs, that field work can be life-changing. Student vets can get summer work at wildlife preserves around the world. They might find themselves tracking elephants in Africa, working with alligators in Florida, or tracking the health of orangutans in Indonesia. Being a wildlife vet means going to where the animals live.

In addition, some people who are already trained vets add wildlife expertise to their skill set. Several agencies offer training in rehabilitation, for example. When animals in the wild are injured, such as when sea birds are hurt by oil spills, vets can help volunteers care for the animals. However, it takes special knowledge to do that safely, so even doctors can go back to school.

Getting a Head Start

*I*t's not too early to start planning for a veterinary career. Taking science and biology classes is a great start, even for high school students. Plus, nearly all veterinary schools require applicants to have at least 400 hours of animal-related experience. Students can start that work in high school or even before. Volunteer at a shelter or wildlife sanctuary near your home. Ask your pet's vet if you can clean cages or sweep during the summer in exchange for watching them work. Some zoos have programs for students, and some veterinary schools even host summer camps for kids. If you attend one of those camps or programs, you may get an opportunity to see actual animal surgeries being performed, learn to treat wounds, or hold a tranquilizer gun. You'll also get experience working with visitors to the park. Some volunteer jobs include giving tours or animal talks.

If you enjoy the volunteer work, then you can start aiming toward veterinary school—and more. Dogs and cats need to be cared for, of course, but for some animal fans, they want to chase the big animals. Such people take the same steps as your veterinarian, but then branch out to learn more . . . and maybe see the world.

You can help a tiny owl as a zoo veterinarian.

 **Text-Dependent Questions**

1. Jeremiah Poghon heads a mobile veterinary unit. Does he take his time heading out to the field when he gets a call? Why or why not?

2. What are some of the topics the students study in veterinary school?

3. Should you make eye contact with a male gorilla? Why or why not?

 **Research Project**

Visit the Web site of the nearest zoo and find out if it hosts summer programs for teens or kids who want to work with animals. What kinds of activities does it offer? How much does it cost to attend? Also, find out what kind of animals are at the zoo and if any are among your favorites.

Tools of the Trade

2

Wildlife veterinarians perform many of the same jobs as doctors who take care of humans. Vets **suture** and bandage wounds, set broken bones, and perform surgery. You might recognize much of a vet's equipment. For example, when a vet needs to listen to an elephant's heart, he or she uses a stethoscope—although it may be an "extended" model, longer than the one you'll see at a doctor's office. Large animals have large hearts . . . and sometimes they are hard to reach.

WORDS TO UNDERSTAND

assess   to determine the condition of someone or something

compressed   describes something that has been pressed together to reduce the size, amount, or volume

diagnose   to recognize by signs and symptoms

suture   the act or process of sewing with sutures, which are threads or fibers used to sew parts of the living body

Key Machines

Like other doctors, wildlife vets also use ultrasound machines, anesthesia machines, and vital-sign monitors. One big difference is that because a wild animal isn't likely to stroll into its veterinarian's office and ask for an exam, much of the equipment must be portable so it can be carried out into the field.

Portable X-ray machines can help take important pictures of animals in the field or in a zoo setting. The vets working with the machine are wearing lead aprons to protect against X-ray exposure.

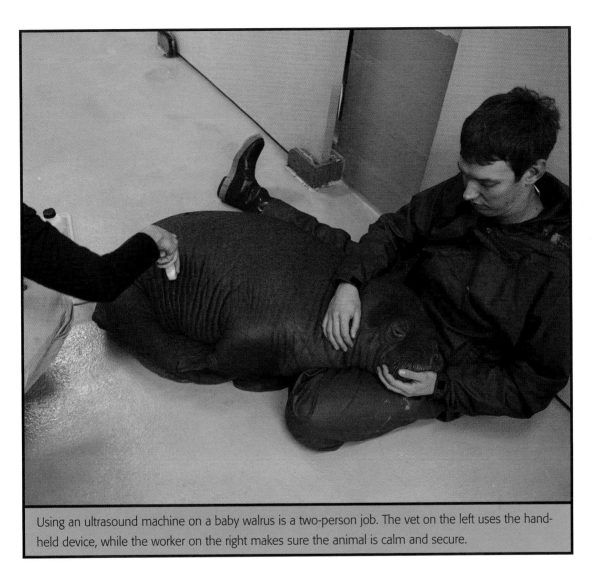

Using an ultrasound machine on a baby walrus is a two-person job. The vet on the left uses the hand-held device, while the worker on the right makes sure the animal is calm and secure.

Ultrasound Equipment: Ultrasound machines direct sound waves to a body part, and the reflection of the sound waves creates an image on a screen. The image is updated hundreds of times per minute. A vet can watch live footage of the body part as it moves and functions. The vet may need to see if a sick gorilla's liver is working properly, check on the progress of a pregnant elephant, or examine a rhino's failing kidneys. Ultrasound technology can help.

X-rays: Wildlife vets use portable X-ray equipment to **diagnose** fractures, find tumors, and see foreign objects that an animal patient may have swallowed. Unlike older models, which used radiation, most X-ray machines are now digital. They provide clearer pictures and allow vets to view the images on a computer or a tablet.

Vital-sign Monitors: Vets need to monitor the patient's temperature, heart rate, blood pressure, and breathing rate. Special machines keep track of those vital signs. New models use wireless signals to transmit the information to specialists in a hospital or lab. That sort of instant advice can be crucial to a wildlife vet working far away from the comfort and safety of an examining room.

While this snow leopard is undergoing an operation, a blood pressure cuff (the black band) provides the vet with information. The plastic cone over the leopard's mouth gives it the anesthesia.

Visitors to Disney's Animal Kingdom ride open cars such as this one. The veterinarians caring for the animals in the park's wide-open spaces also use vehicles to reach their patients.

On steep hills or rough terrain, veterinarians and their helpers must carry their equipment by hand, but some are lucky enough to be able to ride to their patients in fully equipped mobile veterinary units. These vehicles carry everything from an anesthesia machine and portable X-ray and ultrasound units to dart-gun equipment, monitors, dental tools, bandages, and lots more. Veterinarians who work at Disney's Animal Kingdom Theme Park—which houses everything from tiny poison dart frogs to 13,000-pound African elephants—have a state-of-the-art veterinary van. When asked how they get giraffes, rhinos, and other large animals to the hospital, they say, "We don't. We bring the hospital to them."

Sharp Shooters

The darts that vets use to inject medicine from a safe distance also work giving an animal an injection.

One big difference between your doctor and a wildlife veterinarian is that your doctor has probably never shot you with a dart gun or blowpipe. Veterinarians use those devices to immobilize their patients before treating them.

A dart gun uses **compressed** gas—often carbon dioxide—to shoot a dart filled with a tranquilizer into the animal. The drug temporarily puts the animal to sleep so it can be approached by the veterinary team. A blowpipe works the same way, except that the veterinarian uses air from his or her lungs to blow through the pipe. That air pressure shoots the dart. Darts from a blowpipe don't travel as far, but it's a quieter system and not likely to scare an animal as much as the crack from a gun.

The first modern dart gun was invented in the 1950s by Colin Murdoch, a pharmacist and veterinarian from New Zealand. Murdoch was studying wild goats and deer. He realized the animals would be easier to catch, examine, and release if they could be sedated from far away.

Even with the new-and-improved dart guns that have been introduced since then, veterinarians have to practice. It takes good aim to hit an animal with a dart from far away, particularly if the animal is moving. In darting an animal, math is actually one of the most useful sciences. The user of a dart gun or blowpipe must consider how heavy the dart is, how far it must travel, and how fast it will be moving on impact. Is there wind blowing that will affect how the dart flies? How thick is the animal's coat or hide? How dense are its muscles? The dart isn't going to do much good if it's moving too slowly or from too far away to penetrate the thick hide and strong muscles of a massive rhino. Using math and experience, they can answer all those questions to make the perfect shot.

A veterinarian must also try to predict how an animal will land once it's sedated. For example, if a hippo lands with its head lower than the rest of its body, it could suffocate—and it's very hard to reposition a 3,000-pound hippo once it's been sedated. Even where the dart hits on the animal's body matters. Plus, an animal that has been darted could stumble over a cliff or fall into a deep pool of water.

It also takes a lot of skill to know which drugs to use and which dosage is right for the patient. Drug choices are different for every

Don't Blow It

Blowpipes have been around since the Stone Age, when people used hollowed-out reeds and sharp projectiles to hunt. Hunters later discovered that they could tip the projectiles with poisonous substances in order to bring down their prey more easily. In South America, a plant extract called curare was often used. Ninjas in Japan reportedly used poison from the fugu fish on their darts!

species, and sometimes veterinarians face a difficult choice. There is always risk involved in sedating any animal, even healthy ones. All doctors really prefer to examine their patients first to **assess** whether or not they are good candidates for sedation. The only way to do that assessment is to take a blood sample, but that usually can't be done on a wild animal that hasn't been sedated.

Like doctors for people, vets depend on state-of-the-art gear to make sure their patients get the best care.

Once the animal has been safely put to sleep by the dart, doctors can move in and complete the examination. They have to work quickly, though. Keeping animals "out" for too long can harm them.

Text-Dependent Questions

1. Name one of the three portable machines used by wildlife vets.

2. How are current models of X-ray machines different from those used in past decades?

3. How might a stethoscope used by a wildlife vet differ from that used by a doctor who examines humans?

Research Project

Suppose you had to stock a mobile veterinary unit. What kinds of equipment would you include? Where would you buy the equipment?

WORDS TO UNDERSTAND

abscess a collection of pus surrounded by inflamed tissue somewhere in the body

catheter a thin tube that is put into the body to remove or inject a liquid or to keep a passage open

encroach to enter or force oneself on another's property or rights, little by little

hernia the sticking out of an organ or part through connective tissue or through a wall of the cavity in which it is normally enclosed

incision a cut made into the body during surgery

root canal a dental procedure to save a tooth by removing diseased or injured tissue near its root

skin grafts a piece of skin transplanted to a new site on the body

Tales From the Field!

Wildlife vets around the world face unique problems every day. They use their training and experience—and sometimes a little creativity—to bring healing to some of nature's most amazing animals.

Polar Bear Problem

Dr. Jennifer Langan of Chicago's Brookfield Zoo did not have to examine her patient too closely to diagnose the problem. Aussie, a 1,000-pound male polar bear, had a large basketball-like bump emerging from his belly button. It was obviously a **hernia**, which can be a serious issue in any animal. Aussie was clearly in agony, and Langan knew she had to act fast.

She also knew that vets who care for dogs and cats repaired hernias all the time—but never on a patient as large as Aussie. Maybe pooling their knowledge would be a good idea. She made a call, and within hours doctors from the nearby University of Illinois College of Veterinary Medicine were on their way to Chicago.

Meanwhile, Langan was faced with the problem of moving Aussie from his habitat to the medical facility through a zoo crowded with visitors. If

Moving a large and heavy polar bear from a zoo enclosure like this one in Chicago into an operating room took some creative thinking on the part of the big animal vets.

she didn't dose him with enough anesthetic and he woke up during the ride, he might cause chaos. Langan took careful aim and darted Aussie in the right shoulder; he was in so much pain from the hernia that he barely reacted and was soon sleeping peacefully. Twenty zookeepers helped the vet lift Aussie onto a forklift. Then the forklift driver lowered the bear onto the back of a truck. Hundreds of visitors lined the zoo's walkways to watch the 20-year-old bear make the trip to the operating room. That was certainly something none of them had ever seen before. Meanwhile, Langan was squashed between the wet, smelly bear and the side of the truck, hoping that the dosage was right.

Aussie's surgery went well, thanks to the help of the small-animal doctors. He was soon back in his habitat, eating well and playing in his ice-cold pool. Now when he does a belly flop, his belly is free of painful hernias.

The Root of the Problem

Dr. Susan Mikota and veterinary dental technician Michael McCullar were invited to the National Zoo in El Salvador to care of Alfredito. The hippo had broken off his lower right tusk at the gum line. The vets knew they would be in for a challenge. They could see

Hippos have only a few teeth, so taking care of even one of them is important. All of their teeth are very sharp and used mostly for defense or pulling grasses from the bottom of rivers.

from pictures that the nerves and blood vessels inside the tooth were totally exposed. The injury called for a procedure called a **root canal**. As far as they knew, however, no one had ever attempted to perform the painful procedure on a hippo.

This happened in the early 1990s, when El Salvador was in the middle of a civil war. The vets realized that supplies might be difficult to find there. They carefully packed everything they thought they might need—syringes, dental tools, drugs, and a dart-gun system—and headed off. Before they even arrived at the zoo, their troubles began.

The Bronx Zoo's gorilla, Holli, was a healthy captive primate, much like this animal . . . until Holli got very sick and big-animal vets had to work quickly to save her life.

At the airport in San Salvador, the country's capital, they faced a customs inspector, who eyed their dart gun and syringes with suspicion. Mikota explained in Spanish that the dart gun was used to anesthetize animals, saying, "Este rifle es para animales. Para anesthesia." Still, the uniformed man looked distrustful. She tried again, "*Por favor, señor. Esté es para ayudar Alfredito, el hipo.*" ("Please, sir. This is to help Alfredito, the hippo.")

As soon as the official heard Alfredito's name, he smiled warmly. Many Salvadorans had heard of the beloved hippo's injury and worried about him. Mikota and McCullar were ushered immediately through customs and rushed to the zoo. There, a large crowd of onlookers and reporters watched them dart Alfredito. The doctors skillfully removed the damaged tissue from around the root of his tooth, and gave him a dose of antibiotics to avoid infection. As they finished, the onlookers cheered. The next day, the story was in all the local newspapers. (Later, a children's book was written about their mission of mercy.) The pair were later invited back to El Salvador to perform root canals on almost 20 other animals, including four leopards, a lion, and a grizzly bear.

Creativity in Action

It had been a rough few weeks for Holli, a 180-pound female gorilla from the Bronx Zoo. She had stopped eating and become sad and slow. Vets did some tests and found a deep **abscess** in her abdomen. They successfully operated, removing part of her colon, but that was only the start of a long recuperation process that required Holli to remain in the zoo's 30,000-square-foot health center.

Her vets had a rough time because Holli was not a cooperative patient. She yanked out the stitches from her 10-inch-long

incision and repeatedly ripped out the **catheter** in her arm. That thin tube gave her needed fluids and medicine. When she got bored, she had tantrums and flung around the fresh produce zookeepers brought her. She spit at anyone who approached her, and generally made a mess of her hospital enclosure. Holli and the vets were both relieved when she was well enough to return to her usual home—the zoo's popular 6.5-acre Congo exhibit.

Holli still needed to take medicine for a while longer. This time, it meant she had to take pills. The vets, however, soon found that she was just spitting them out. So they chopped the pills into small pieces. They removed peanuts from the end of the peanut shells, and snuck bits of pill into the shells. Because Holli loved peanuts, she gobbled them up without complaint. Veterinarians can be tricky when the situation calls for it!

Team Effort

Veterinarians at the Houston Zoo were stumped. Cheyenne, a 42-year-old orangutan, was not her usual lovable self. She had stopped eating and was spending her days slumped in her enclosure. Blood tests showed she might have an infection.

The vets knew a lot about orangutans, but this looked like a complicated situation. The illness involved different organs and systems, and they needed all the help they could get. Humans and orangutans share many characteristics because they are both primates. So the veterinarians turned to doctors at Baylor College of Medicine and Texas Children's Hospital. Working as a team, doctors and vets performed exploratory surgery. They discovered that the orangutan had many problems, including with her liver and kidneys. They needed to figure out a way to give her regular doses of medicine through a tube, but not one that she would pull out, which could kill her. So they came up with a smaller tube. Experts from the children's hospital put it in her ankle. Then they watched her around the clock for two weeks while the medicines took effect.

Cheyenne rested on a comfortable cushioned bed, drinking fruit juice and milkshakes through a straw. After the tube was removed, she returned to her enclosure for a joyful reunion with her fellow

Working with an orangutan like this one, vets at a Houston zoo called on some doctors that normally work on a different kind of primate: human beings.

orangutans. The doctors returned to their non-furry patients. The vets at the Houston Zoo know they can always count on their human doctor counterparts when they need a specialist. Other doctors who have helped out at the zoo include an orthopedist who helped a tiger with a bad elbow and a chiropractor who treated a limping komodo dragon.

Nose Job

Dr. William Fowlds looked down in dismay at a South African rhino named Thandi. The rhino was alive, but just barely. In the center of her face was a gaping, bloody hole. Poachers had brutally sliced off her horn and left her for dead.

Rhino horn is highly prized in some cultures, particularly in Asia. There, it is ground into powder or made into tablets as a treatment for a wide variety of maladies, such as nosebleeds, fevers, and seizures. There is no real scientific evidence that it works, but hundreds of rhinos are killed each year by poachers, who illegally sell the horns to meet the growing demand.

Thandi had been gravely injured in an attack at Kariega Game Reserve that had killed two other rhinos. Fowlds was determined to do everything he could to help. Along with a team of other veterinarians—and a plastic surgeon—he spent more than a year experimenting with ways to repair the damage. Could new rhino skin be created by using **skin grafts**?

Over the course of several months, Thandi underwent several procedures. Small patches of skin from behind her ear and on her neck were grafted onto her wound. She rubbed off much of the new tissue by scratching it on the ground and rolling in the mud. Still, Fowlds has never given up. He'll continue to try new grafting techniques, he has said, and is thinking of ways to create a hard, protective covering to allow the fragile grafts time to grow and get stronger.

Meanwhile, Thandi is not letting her injury stop her from leading a contented life. In 2015, she gave birth to a healthy calf and is living peacefully at a game reserve in South Africa.

One World, One Health

*D*r. Jonathan Epstein isn't just a veterinarian; he's also an epidemiologist, an expert in the branch of medical science that deals with how diseases occur, spread, and can be controlled. That might seem like an odd combination until you consider that some ailments

Vets search for connections between humans and other animals. This species of horseshoe bat turned out to be one of the causes of a virus outbreak in Asia.

Vets working with One Health are exploring ways that animals interact with humans, such as these people on safari in Tanzania. Knowing we have to share the planet, we should know our neighbors!

spread from animals to humans. Because of this, it's important to have people who understand both animal health and human health. Epstein is part of One Health, a global movement that knows that all creatures on the planet are interconnected in important ways.

Working with the EcoHealth Alliance, Epstein was among the first scientists ever to connect the SARS virus, which caused a global epidemic in 2003, to horseshoe bats. The EcoHealth Alliance, according to its Web site, "leads cutting edge research into the critical connections between human and wildlife health and delicate ecosystems." The group uses that research to promote conservation and help stop the spread of disease.

Epstein is now studying Ebola, a virus that people can catch when they eat an infected animal. Once a human catches Ebola, others can get it through direct contact with the sick person's blood or other body fluids. Thousands of people died in Africa during an outbreak in 2014.

Epstein realizes it's sometimes scary to read about diseases such as SARS and Ebola. However, he believes that we need to think calmly about how we develop and farm our land, build our cities, cut down our forests, and take our vacations. The more we **encroach** on wildlife, he explains, the more opportunity there is for a disease that used to exist solely in animals to spread to people. He spends his days thinking not about just one patient but about health on a much broader scale. Epstein thinks that's the future of wildlife medicine. Staying tucked away in a medical facility or lab might soon be a thing of the past. In the future, he predicts, every veterinarian will have to be a "Scientist in Action."

Text-Dependent Questions

1. In what country did veterinarians help Alfredito the hippo? What was his problem?
2. Why do some people buy rhino horns?
3. How did her caretakers get Holli the gorilla to take her pills?

Research Project

Thandi the rhino was a victim of poaching. Go online and find out what other species are targets for poachers. What can be done to stop the poachers? Create a poster that you can hang up in your school telling other kids about the issue.

Scientists in the News

Smile for the Camera: Linda Dixon Reeve grew up on a farm around animals. Today, she and her husband, James Peddie (who also is a veterinarian), put animals in the movies. They care for animals that worked in Hollywood, including gorillas, monkeys, lions, tigers, wolves, and elephants. Because movies are often filmed all over the world, one of Reeve's areas of expertise has become dealing with the regulations and quarantine issues of moving animals between the United States and foreign countries. (Quarantine means a waiting period to make sure a person or an animal does not have a particular disease.) She is also an expert at diagnosing and treating tuberculosis in elephants. Of the many animals she has worked with over the course of her career, only one has ever injured her badly: As a young vet, she was kicked by a cow!

The Minds of Animals: All vets know how to take care of a physically sick animal, but there are some vets whose job is to tend to the mental health of their patients, too. Dr. Vint Virga is a veterinarian and animal behaviorist who can tell what it means when a hippo rapidly flips its tail or a giraffe refuses to eat. Just like us, he explains, animals get depressed, worried, and emotional. Virga consults with zoos across the country. After observing an animal that is behaving oddly, he decides whether it needs to be trained in a different way, have its habitat changed, or take medicine such as antidepressants. When scientists say that we don't know how animals feel because they can't tell us, he replies that we're just not listening well enough.

It's a (Very) Small World: Dr. Oliver Ryder has a degree in biology rather than veterinary medicine, but he oversees one of the most unusual zoos around. San Diego's Frozen Zoo is not a place you'd visit to watch playful chimpanzees swinging on vines or lions prowling majestically through their habitat. Instead, Ryder oversees a collection of cells that have been taken from more than 1,000 species and placed in cold storage, in vats of liquid nitrogen. Already, scientists working at the Frozen Zoo have generated stem cells from the endangered northern white rhino.

Samples from the Frozen Zoo help preserve species for the future.

There are only a few white rhinos left in the world, so they hope the cells can be used to expand the rhinos' gene pool and save them from extinction. It has been proven in the lab that a single stem cell from a mouse can direct the development of a whole new mouse, so Frozen Zoo researchers might be able to help create new herds of rhinos one day.

Find Out More

Books

Karesh, William B. *Appointment at the Ends of the World: Memoirs of a Wildlife Veterinarian.* New York: Warner Books, reprint edition, 2009.

Pattengale, Paula and Sonsthagen, Teresa. *Tasks for the Veterinary Assistant.* Hoboken, N.J.: Wiley-Blackwell, 2014.

Spelman, Lucy. *National Geographic Animal Encyclopedia: 2,500 Animals With Photos, Maps, and More!* Washington, D.C.: National Geographic Books for Children, 2012.

Web Sites

kids.nationalgeographic.com/
National Geographic Kids

www.aavmc.org/Students-Applicants-and-Advisors.aspx
Association of American Veterinary Medical Colleges

www.vetmed.ucdavis.edu/vmth/large_animal/index.cfm
University of California—Davis, one of the U.S.'s biggest vet schools

Series Glossary of Key Terms

airlock   a room on a space station from which astronauts can move from inside to outside the station and back

anatomy   a branch of knowledge that deals with the structure of organisms

bionic   to be assisted by mechanical movements

carbon dioxide   a gas that is in the air that we breathe out

classified   kept secret from all but a few people in a government or an organization

deforestation   the destruction of forest or woodland

diagnose   to recognize by signs and symptoms

discipline   in science, this means a particular field of study

elite   the part or group having the highest quality or importance

genes   information stored in cells that determine a person's physical characteristics

geostationary   remaining in the same place above the Earth during an orbit

innovative   groundbreaking, original

inquisitiveness   an ability to be curious, to continue asking questions to learn more

internships   jobs often done for free by people in the early stages of study for a career

marine   having to do with the ocean

meteorologist   a scientist who forecasts weather and weather patterns

physicist   a scientist who studies physics, which examines how matter and energy move and relate

primate   a type of four-limbed mammal with a developed brain; includes humans, apes, and monkeys

traits   a particular quality or personality belonging to a person

Index

Photo Credits

Dreamstime.com: Sergieiev 7; Hungchungchih 15; Stefano Panzeri 19; Pleprakaymas 20; Jiawangkun 27; Kittycat 32; Asiavasmuncky 34; Kerstiny 35; Evantravels 36; Xian Zhang 39; Dennis Donohue 41; Boaz Yunior Wibowo 45.

Courtesy of Dr. Michael Cranfield: 9, 10; DollarPhoto: Phloxii 12; Newscom/KRT/Stuart Wong: 16; Shutterstock/Chameleoneye: 18; Adi Ciurea 42; Mike Eliason: 22, 26, 28; Smithsonian National Zoo: 24; Newscom/Anchorage Daily News/Marc Lester: 25; Newscom/Philadelphia Inquirer/Michael Plunkett: 30.

Scientists in Action logo by Comicraft.

About the Author

Mari Rich was educated at Lehman College, part of the public City University of New York. As a writer and editor, she has had many years of experience in the fields of university communications and reference publishing, most notably with the highly regarded periodical *Current Biography*, aimed at high school and college readers. She also edited and wrote for *World Authors, Leaders of the Information Age,* and *Nobel Laureates.* Currently, she spends much of her time writing about engineers and engineering.